INCLINED PLANES

A Buddy Book

by

SARAH TIECK

ABDO
Publishing Company

VISIT US AT
www.abdopublishing.com

Published by ABDO Publishing Company, 4940 Viking Drive, Edina, Minnesota 55435.

Copyright © 2007 by Abdo Consulting Group, Inc. International copyrights reserved in all countries. No part of this book may be reproduced in any form without written permission from the publisher. Buddy Books™ is a trademark and logo of ABDO Publishing Company.

Printed in the United States.

Contributing Editor: Michael P. Goecke
Graphic Design: Maria Hosley
Cover Photograph: Photos.com, Clipart.com
Interior Photographs/Illustrations: Clipart.com, Flatearth, Photodisc, Photos.com

Special thanks to Fred Heim.

Library of Congress Cataloging-in-Publication Data

Tieck, Sarah, 1976–
    Inclined planes / Sarah Tieck.
        p. cm. — (Simple machines)
    Includes index.
    ISBN-13: 978-1-59679-818-2
    ISBN-10: 1-59679-818-1
    1. Inclined planes—Juvenile literature. I. Title. II. Series: Tieck, Sarah, 1976- Simple machines.

TJ147.T484 2006
621.8—dc22

                                                                2006010047

Table Of Contents

What Is An Inclined Plane?

Inclined planes are used to move heavy loads. An inclined plane is a simple machine. A simple machine has few moving parts, sometimes only one.

Simple machines give people a **mechanical advantage**. This is how inclined planes help make work easier for people.

A skate ramp is an example of an inclined plane.

Inclined planes are not the only simple machines. There are six simple machines. These include inclined planes, wedges, levers, pulleys, screws, and wheels and axles.

Sometimes, simple machines work together. Most machines are made up of more than one simple machine. Examples of inclined planes include skateboard ramps, stairs, and ladders.

simple machines

Inclined Planes
Help move objects.

Levers
Help lift or move objects.

Pulleys
Help move, lift, and lower objects.

Screws
Help lift, lower, and fasten objects.

Wedges
Help fasten or split objects.

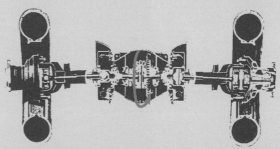

Wheels and Axles
Help move objects.

Parts Of An Inclined Plane

The design of an inclined plane helps people move objects. Lifting is not necessary with an inclined plane. Instead a person can push a heavy object up or down using this simple machine. Inclined planes give people a mechanical advantage.

Vertical Rise

Angle of Incline

Length of Incline

The stairway up to this airplane is an inclined plane. Stairs help make the angle less steep.

An inclined plane is a flat surface that is tilted at an **angle**. One end is higher than the other. This forms a **gradual** angle. The load is the machine's moving part.

An inclined plane helps make it easier to move a load. The inclined plane changes the amount of force that is needed.

The inclined plane does not move. Someone or something must supply force to the load to make this tool work. This force is what makes the load move up or down. The person may need to move the load farther, but less force is needed.

An inclined plane helps people move a load of boxes into a truck.

How Does An Inclined Plane Work?

It is not easy for a person to lift something heavy, such as a barrel, on his or her own. But, a person could move a barrel using an inclined plane. This is because inclined planes make work easier.

To use an inclined plane to move a barrel, a person would place the barrel at the bottom of the inclined plane. Next, they would push the barrel up the slope.

A shorter ramp has a steeper angle and requires more effort.

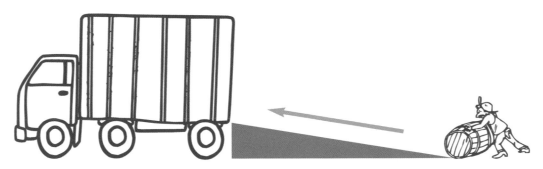

A longer ramp has a gradual angle and requires less effort.

The longer the ramp, the easier it is to move the barrel. A longer ramp gives a greater mechanical advantage.

Different Inclined Planes At Work

There are many different ways to use an inclined plane. It is possible to change an inclined plane's shape. People also change its size and angle. These changes help inclined planes perform different jobs. Because of this, inclined planes have many uses.

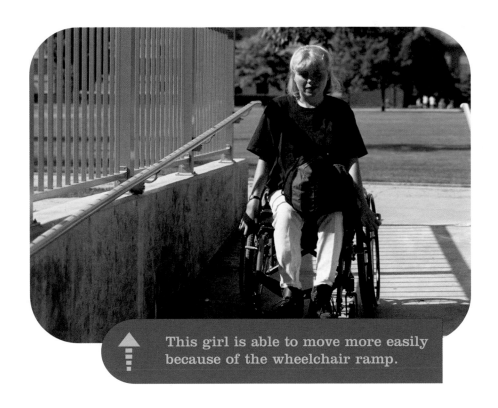

This girl is able to move more easily because of the wheelchair ramp.

A wheelchair ramp is an inclined plane. The longer the ramp, the less force is needed to move a wheelchair.

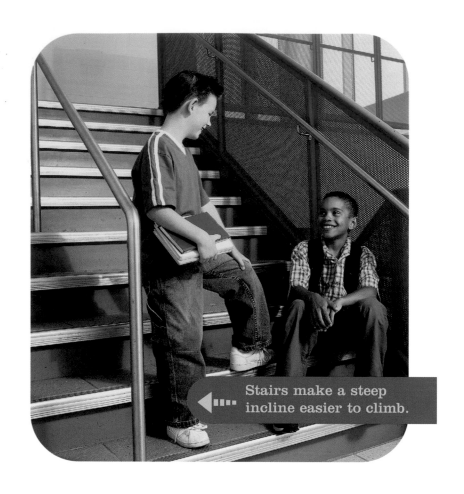

Stairs make a steep incline easier to climb.

A staircase is also an inclined plane. It is used instead of a steep ramp. This lets people move from a lower level to a higher level more easily.

The roof of this house has many parts. They are all inclined planes.

The roof of a house can also be an inclined plane. Snow, water, and other objects slide off of a steep roof. This helps protect the house.

The History Of Inclined Planes

The inclined plane has been used for many years. It was one of the first tools.

In ancient times, people made many things by hand. It is said that ancient Egyptians used inclined planes to help build pyramids. They used inclined planes to help move giant stones into place.

In early times, people didn't have machines with motors. They had to do work with their bodies.

The inclined plane helped make their work easier. This tool is still used today.

How Do Inclined Planes Help People Today?

Today people have many types of tools. But, they still use inclined planes. When you climb a ladder, you are using an inclined plane. You are also using an inclined plane when you ride up or down a sloping road in a car. When you slide down a slide, you are using another inclined plane.

20

A ladder is an inclined plane. It helps people to do work more easily.

This winding mountain road is an example of an inclined plane.

Inclined planes help with many different jobs all over the world.

Web Sites

To learn more about **Inclined Planes**, visit ABDO Publishing Company on the World Wide Web. Web site links about **Inclined Planes** are featured on our Book Links page. These links are routinely monitored and updated to provide the most current information available.

www.abdopublishing.com

Important Words

angle the shape made by two straight lines or surfaces meeting in a point.

distance how far the load moves.

effort an attempt to lift or move something.

force a push or pull against resistance.

gradual a little bit at a time.

load the object that needs to be turned, lifted, or moved.

mechanical advantage the way simple machines make work easier. Using a simple machine to help with a task means less, or different, force is needed to do a job. The same job would require more force without the help of a simple machine.

resistance something that works against or opposes.

Index